Joy Worthy

The Little Guide to Experiencing All

the Joy you Deserve

Joy Worthy

The Little Guide to Experiencing All the Joy You Deserve

Dr. Latoya Bosworth

Edited by Tianna Glass-Tripp

Cover Photo by Keith Claytor

©2024 Brenda's Child for Two Two INK

All rights reserved. No part of this book may be reproduced, stored in a retrieval system or transmitted in any form or any means without prior written consent of the publisher. ISBN 978-1-304-15478-1

Dedicated to the younger versions of myself, who were afraid to feel joy and didn't feel worthy.

To my current self, who knows she was always worthy and is now actively increasing her capacity for joy.

To my future self, who is committed to experiencing all of the joy she can handle with every single breath.

Joy Worthy…

1. Joy in the Moment

2. Joy in Solitude

3. Joy in Times of Sadness

4. Joy is in Connecting

5. Joy in the morning

Affirmations for Joy

"Joy is a freedom. It helps a person to find his/her own liberation. The person who is joyous takes responsibility for the time he/she takes up and the space that he/she occupies. You share it! Some of you have it…you share it! That is what joy is! When you continue to give it away you will still have so much more of it."

-Maya Angelou

Introduction

Joy *verb.* To experience great pleasure or delight (Merriam Webster).

Synonyms *Exuberate, jubilate, rejoice*

Joy is not the same thing as laughter. Joy can be exuberant but doesn't necessarily have to be high-spirited. Joy is *not* the same thing as happiness. Unlike happiness, which is heavily influenced by external factors, joy comes from within. Joy is subjective. However it manifests, joy is holistically beneficial. A joyful existence positively supports our nervous system, our immune system, our heart health, our mental health, our overall well-being, and our chances for increased longevity.

Multiple factors, many of which we cannot control, influence our ability to experience joy; genetics, environment, self-awareness, and past trauma. In this book, we will talk about what we can control, specifically our perspectives, our intentions, and our ability to choose. Ultimately choosing joy requires shifts in our thoughts and actions, and sometimes that can feel like work. I would be hustling you if I said it was always easy. It certainly isn't. But it's worth it because you are worth it.

Joy is actually connected to worthiness. We have to feel we are worthy of joy to be open to feeling it. Sometimes our lived experiences suggest to our subconscious that we aren't worthy of joy; that if we allow ourselves to feel it for even a moment, another experience will come and steal it again. We avoid joy because it is fleeting.

The idea for this book actually came to me after a shift in my own perspective of joy and time. There was a period in my life when I saw no purpose in buying flowers. I had a disdain for the idea of flower bouquets. Why waste money on something that would just die? Why not buy a plant instead? They last longer and you can propagate them for more.

It wasn't until a team I supervised bought me a bouquet for Valentine's Day that I began to enjoy flowers. We had bonded deeply under the stress of special education, vicarious trauma, and racial biases. This giving of flowers was a literal and metaphorical symbol of appreciation and love from a team with whom I worked hard to create cohesiveness and trust. I placed the bouquet in my office to show my gratitude. Each day I went in, I looked for them first. They were colorful and brightened my mood. I took care of them, adding the food, and making sure they had plenty of water. They lasted about two weeks before I had to get rid of them. Instead of focusing on the death of the flowers like I used to, I focused on the joy they brought to my days. Lucky for me my team gave me some again for my birthday, and again for Teacher Appreciation Week in May. I came to enjoy flowers so much that I began to buy them for myself at home. I realized that just because something is temporary, doesn't make it any less beautiful and that plants also die eventually. As do all living things. The hack is taking in all in while it's here.

You are here. Take it all in. You deserve it.

Joy in the Moment

"You are the sky. Everything else is just the weather."

- Pema Chödrön

Joy in the moment

Experiencing joy requires that we be willing to surrender. It is being aware of what we truly have control over: how we respond. This can be hard, particularly if you've experienced a significant amount of trauma because feeling like we have a sense of control equates to a greater sense of psychological safety. According to the American Psychological Association (APA) a trauma is "any **disturbing** experience that results in **significant** fear, helplessness, dissociation, confusion, or other **disruptive** feelings **intense** enough to have a **long-lasting negative effect** on a person's attitudes, behavior, and other aspects of **functioning.**" I describe trauma in terms of a mathematical problem:

Harm (caused by people, nature, circumstance, culture) + Helplessness (not in control) = A changed perception of what feels safe.

Whether we have normalized or recognized a traumatic experience, our bodies and brains will start to operate in ways that make us feel safe. For many trauma survivors, our way of being shifts to a need to control. Feeling like we have command of a situation gives us an imagined sense of security.

Equally, if we are used to having a sense of power or privilege, we also want to be in control. In reality, what we have true control over is minimal. Even with ourselves, we often don't have as much control as we'd like to believe.

For instance, intrusive thoughts and emotions can flood our minds and bodies at the most inopportune times. All we have is what we choose to do with them. And sometimes the only thing we can do is surrender.

To surrender is *not* to give up; it is to allow the occurrence of whatever is supposed to happen. It requires trust, and trust requires faith in something bigger than you. More importantly, concern for the how and the why has to be surrendered as well. I'll discuss this more in a later chapter. For now, let's talk about choosing joy in the moment.

Being stuck on the Massachusetts Turnpike in bumper-to-bumper traffic is a consistent lesson for me. When I hear the GPS tell me that traffic is getting worse or that there is an 18-minute slowdown, I surrender. I don't know what I'm being protected from, or aligned with, so I choose joy. I decide to listen to Whitney Houston's *How Will I Know*, sing at the top of my lungs and dance (as much as I can when I'm constrained by a seat belt). I care not even a little bit about the people who may be looking or judging, because I know what I'm *not* doing: I'm not allowing cortisol to rush through my body, my face is not wrinkled in frustration, I'm not banging on the steering wheel or beeping my horn fruitlessly. I am having a few moments of bliss because that is what I can choose to control.

In frustrating moments, try one or more of the 4 A's:

1. **Affirm Yourself:** I am exactly where I'm supposed to be right now.
2. **Ask:** What about this situation can I control?

(The answer isn't NOTHING, because again you have your autonomy: you can control you!) How can I shift my perspective and mood to joyfulness? Then do it.
3. **Assess:** What can I be grateful for in this moment? Name it and say thank you.
4. **Alert:** Remind yourself to be here (even if you'd rather be elsewhere). This can be done by connecting with your body; try clapping your hands, stomping your feet, or tapping your heart or belly.

To get to a place where you can more easily shift to joy, it requires commitment and experimentation. First, you have to be committed to choosing not to stay angry or frustrated, and to wanting to change how you feel. Secondly, you have to be open to trying new things that will facilitate joyful experiences.

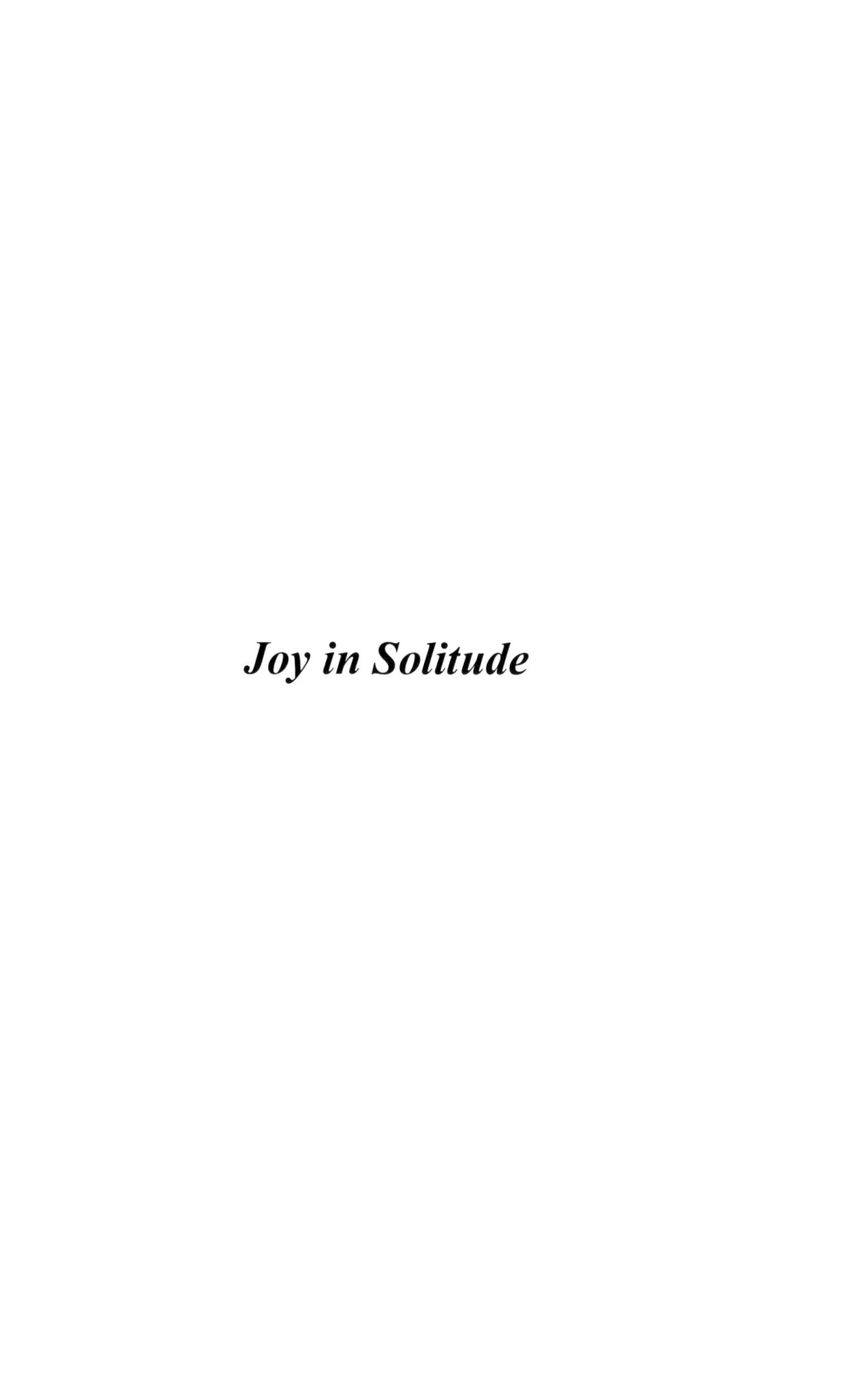

Joy in Solitude

Knowing how to be solitary is central to the art of loving. When we can be alone, we can be with others without using them as a means of escape."

– Bell Hooks

Joy in Solitude

When you are watching TV or scrolling on your phone, you are not really alone. You are connecting through other people's experiences. You are still engaging. But when you are truly alone, you are able to take notice of a need you have, such as rest, or you notice that you've been missing parts of your body when you moisturize because you've been moving too quickly. You may notice your emotions and then give yourself permission to feel them freely, without judgment from others and then you stop judging yourself. You actually begin to enjoy the quiet; the sensation of not using your throat, lips, and tongue to speak. We only offer rest to our vocal cords when we are sleeping (especially if you're Black, because you know we love to talk to the screen when watching movies).

Joy in solitude is learning to reconnect with our bodies more intimately. I'm not just talking about intimacy through masturbation. We become more intimate in the sense that we move from noticing to appreciating what our bodies can do; all they've endured. Joy in solitude allows us to be grateful and sentient.

When we aren't listening to others, we can hear ourselves. That is what mindfulness is: being in the moment, aware of what is happening now. We become more sensitive to sensation. Our hearing, our sense of touch, taste and smell are all heightened when we aren't distracted by others. It's why I love dining alone; I eat slower and less. I enjoy every flavor. Although I'd love to text someone about how good it is, I resist the urge.

Yet, there are so many people who won't dine or go to a movie alone because it feels awkward, or they fear they may look lonely or silly. If this is you, that's even more a reason you should do it. Outside of trauma, being comfortable alone is something we should actively challenge ourselves to do. There is so much benefit from learning to connect with ourselves daily and often.

Ten Things to Joyfully Do on Your Own

1. Take a cooking or pottery class.
2. Movement – yoga, dance, boxing, walking.
3. Go to a festival or concert.
4. Visit a museum.
5. Go to the beach.
6. Go to a park.
7. Take a short road trip.
8. Visit a coffee or ice cream shop.
9. Go to a play.
10. Have a spa day (at home or at a salon).

Joy in Times of Sadness

"A life with love will have some thorns, but a life without love will have no roses."
-Anonymous

Joy in Times of Sadness

In the darkest times, joy has long served as a form of resistance for my African and Indigenous ancestors. They were stolen and robbed of their homeland, and their resources continue to be stolen today. Our children, our elders, our rights, our religion, all stolen; our culture exploited, vilified, and appropriated. But through it all, our joy has remained. Our joy is both spontaneous and deliberate, quiet and loud, in public and private, in solitude and in community. Sometimes it's exuberant and in celebration, and sometimes it's laughter or feelings of gratitude through tears of sorrow. To the outside world, it can look inappropriate to make eye contact and giggle in unison at someone's less-than-stellar singing during a funeral service or catch a glimpse of ourselves crying in the mirror and laugh at how dry our lips may be. To us, it is survival. Experiencing joy through pain is our protective factor. Actively seeking joy in times of grief can feel misaligned. There is a threat of judgment from others and ourselves. We've been told that we should be sad because if joy and laughter exist, then the grief we feel is invalid. But more than one thing can be true at a time.

A more recent example of this in my life was the day my paternal great-aunt transitioned. It was surreal, out of body. Her passing was impending, so it wasn't shock I was feeling. It was re-experiencing a previous trauma. It was November and my great-aunt had ovarian cancer. Exactly 30 years before, my maternal grandmother, who had been my caregiver since I was four, was also dying of ovarian cancer. The last Thanksgiving she was alive was the first one she hadn't cooked for since I could remember. She would transition a month later, on Christmas.

Although I was at my great-aunts' house, I was taken back to being 12 years old; watching adults comfort each other, and gather in the kitchen to reminisce, to shift from moments of heavy silence to outbursts of laughter through watery eyes. Except I wasn't twelve, I was a grown woman, who became a witness, an observer of my experience. Taking it all in, I noticed my little cousin, who was about 10 years old. She sat alone in the living room, quietly sobbing. I saw my young self in her. The adults in the room were comforting each other, consumed with their own grief, and I saw a moment to make her grief experience different from mine.

When my grandmother transitioned, I also experienced adults comforting each other with company, conversation, and laughter, and then I saw them move on abruptly in what was an attempt to normalize Christmas morning. My grandmother died at 9:30am and by mid-afternoon, we were opening presents like we hadn't all been unanchored by the loss of our matriarch. I wrote about those feelings in my 2010 memoir, *The Right Amount of Sunshine…Cultivating Little Girls into Young Ladies:*

I remember I got a diary on that Christmas morning. This would be the first time I would begin to put my thoughts on paper. It was one of those small diaries, with the flap that locked closed with a set of gold keys. I don't know whatever happened to that particular diary, but I remember its first entry; it was angry. I remember writing that I wanted to scream at all of the adults in the room, "She's dead! She's dead! Stop pretending to be happy!"

The following holiday season, we began exchanging gifts on Christmas Eve, and everyone did their own thing on Christmas Day. There was no conversation or explanation of the shift, just a shift. What I took from that was that emotional pain – sadness, grief, fear about what was next – was something you kept to yourself, because it makes people feel uncomfortable. I kept them inside for years.

More than 30 years later, I saw an opportunity to give my little cousin something I wasn't afforded: I held space for her. Acknowledged her grief. We took a walk outside; I listened to and affirmed her beliefs about what happens when we die. She would still have a relationship with her great-grandmother, but it would look different; she would send her signs to let her know that she was still around and still loved her. On our way back to the house, she found a leaf on the sidewalk; it was heart shaped. She picked it up and said, "You think this is a sign from her?" I said, "absolutely." I couldn't erase all the pain. She will forever have moments where grief overwhelms her. But she'd also have a soft, safe space to share her emotions.

Later that day, I held my grandmother's hand while they carried her sister's body past us down the stairs. I couldn't help thinking, *what a full circle moment*. Grandmothers are usually the ones who comfort their grandchildren to make them feel safe. But I was blessed that she was alive and healthy enough for the inevitable role reversal. While I held her hand, I continued to witness. I watched my cousin: he was my aunt's last-born child. She was there when he took his first breath, and he stayed until she took her last. As he cried, one of his sons placed his arms around his shoulder and became his strength, another full circle moment.

Through my own grief and re-experiencing trauma, I was still able to soak in the beauty of the moment. In challenging times, we are encouraged to lean into our faith in knowing that something better is to come. I encourage you to go one step further and find the beauty, and the gratitude in the moment. Ask yourself, *where is the beauty in this moment even if it's only temporary? What can I be thankful for in this difficult moment?* Joy in the midst of sorrow isn't about pretending we aren't experiencing it, or ignoring our pain, it is surrender. It is a reminder of the brevity of life, and the many beautiful moments we get to experience when we allow ourselves to be present and give ourselves permission to feel joy, even in the midst of death and transition.

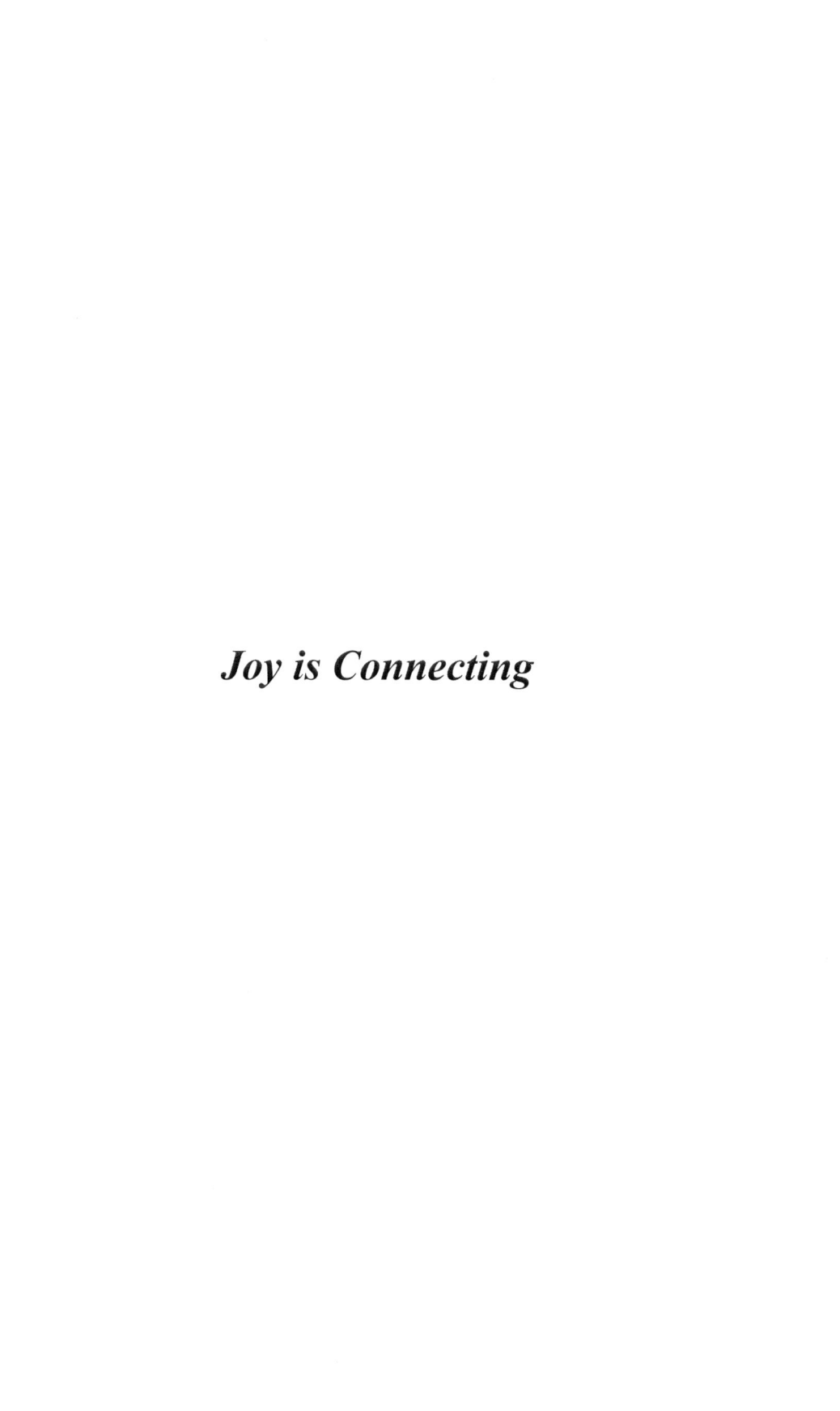

Joy is Connecting

The sharing of joy, whether physical, emotional, psychic, or intellectual, forms a bridge between the sharers which can be the basis for understanding much of what is not shared between them, and lessens the threat of their difference.

-Audre Lorde

Joy is Connecting

As humans, we require connections of various kinds. In this chapter, I'll discuss four types of connection. The first is human connection and community. There are many types of communities – geographic, occupational, religious, and interest-based are just a few. What we know about community, specifically for historically excluded groups, is that it creates a sense of psychological safety, reduces stress, and boosts confidence.

Our connections correlate with our health and well-being whether we acknowledge it or not, whether we notice it or not. While human connection can be emotional, social, and/or physical, it affects our psychological and physiological processes.

We know that some relationships promote stress. This is where you have control. You cannot choose who you are related to, and you may not be able to choose your coworkers, but you do have authority over how and the level that you interact with them. Just as you determine the algorithm of your social media timelines based on what you view and respond to, you can determine your real-life community. Sometimes joy requires that we set boundaries, distance ourselves, and risk feeling like we are being "mean." This is the hard part; the risk of your intentions being misunderstood.

In my book *Quiet Strength, Loud Confidence, Reflections and Realization from a Free Black Woman*, I write about the "backlash" from setting boundaries:

Anytime you decide to set boundaries with people in your life, whether personal or professional, you must prepare yourself for the imminent backlash. It will come. We are creatures of habit; when you decide to change how you interact with someone, it rattles them. They are shocked, offended, confused, and instantly make it about them. What do they do? Why are you treating them like this? You've always allowed this; why are you changing now? If you are not careful, you could wind up being manipulated or guilt-tripped into compromising those newly set boundaries.

Ultimately you will have to choose between the temporary conflict and discomfort of standing in your truth, or the lasting mental and physical harm caused by forcing toxic, chaotic connections. What is long-term peace, health, and joy worth to you?

If unhealthy connections increase our stress levels, then positive, loving connections increase our joy. It's not just how we connect, it's also with whom we connect. Our bodies do a premier job of telling us who we should be connecting to if we are willing to listen. Pay attention to how people make you feel when you are with them, in anticipation of being with them, and after you leave them. Emotionally – Do you feel safe? Loved? Anxious? Physically – How do you feel in your stomach? Your heart? How do your muscles feel? In your shoulders? Your neck? Your jaw? Reflect on these questions in a journal and begin assessing in real time to filter out who supports your joy.

Earlier in the book, I talked about the joy of being alone. Connecting to self is also about re-connecting with the parts of ourselves we've lost or stifled, including our little selves. Who were you before the world told you otherwise? Were you the risktaker? The creative? The gymnast? The action hero? What were your favorite games or toys? Make time to reacquaint yourself with those experiences. Why? Because play boosts your creativity, which can extend to other areas of your life; it releases endorphins, relieves stress, and boosts energy. Don't miss an opportunity to build with Legos, do a cartwheel in the grass, play hopscotch, or freeze tag. Playing is joy in action.

In a world of same-day delivery and artificial intelligence, we have immediate access to everything we want and need with a tap of a button. However, to reap the benefits of the sun, air, earth, and water we have to spend more time outside. Not only does exposure to sunlight boost mood, but newer studies published by the National Institute for Health suggest that lack of sun is detrimental to mental health. Although air pollution has long-term negative effects, being in greener spaces among trees and flowers improves our intake of healthier oxygen. Grounding (skin contact with the earth) has been found to reduce inflammation and improve the immune system. Watching, feeling, and hearing natural waterscapes (rivers, oceans, waterfalls) reduces anxiety. It's simple: nature regulates our entire body. From nerves to hormones to heartbeat; it calms us down, bringing us to the present.

Personally, when I spend time in nature, I tend to receive what I call spiritual downloads – guidance and inspiration. Embracing spirituality supports joy. Notice, I said *spirituality*, and not necessarily religion. Spirituality is a part of religion but can exist outside of it. Religion is organized, with clear leadership and rules; spirituality is fluid, more internally led by the individual. Both are *supposed* to embrace love and compassion; connection to and belief in something outside of ourselves. Whether you call it Great Spirit, God, Jehovah, Allah, or the Universe, spiritually connected people tend to be more optimistic, more resilient... and more joyful.

Connecting in four separate ways can feel overwhelming. I recommend connecting in two or more ways at once. Here are just a few examples.

1. Writing a gratitude list, meditating, or praying outside in the grass or at the beach.
2. Going for a walk with a friend or family member who brings you joy.
3. Playing catch or jump rope outside with a child.
4. Standing barefoot on the earth while talking on the phone to a good friend.
5. Roller skating in your neighborhood.

Joy in the Morning

"A lot of people resist transition and therefore never allow themselves to enjoy who they are.

- Nikki Giovanni

Joy in the Morning (Noon & Night)

Joy cannot wait until the weekend or when you can finally use your PTO. I started this book out with *Joy in the Moment*. Just because it's in the moment doesn't mean we can't make plans to align with the energy of joy. This starts from the instant your day begins. How does it begin? Is it with the blaring sound of a cell phone alarm or a sweet serenade of your favorite song? Each morning presents us with a new opportunity to invite joy into our lives. We can do this through the practice of turning our routines into *rituals*.

Let's examine some definitions of *routines*.

Merriam Webster: *noun.* a regular course of procedure; a habitual or mechanical performance of an established procedure.

Oxford Dictionary: *noun.* a sequence of actions regularly following a fixed program.

Dictionary.com: *noun.* a customary or regular course of procedure; commonplace tasks, chores, or duties that must be done regularly or at specified intervals,

Adjective Form: unvarying, habitual, regular, typical, dull, uninteresting.

What stands out for me first is the descriptor of "mechanical." The image it creates is that of an unfeeling, unthinking machine. The second descriptor of a routine is that rarely changes, it is mundane.

Routines create a sense of psychological safety. Our egos also benefit from routine. We know what to expect, what know what to do. Routines are opportunities for task completion which leaves little room for error, or for personal growth.

Now let's look at the definitions for *ritual*:

Merriam Webster: *noun* a ceremonial act or action regularly repeated in a set precise manner.

Oxford Dictionary: *noun.* a series of actions or types of behavior regularly and invariably followed by someone. a religious or solemn ceremony consisting of a series of actions performed according to a prescribed order.

Dictionary.com: *noun.* prescribed, established, or ceremonial acts, a system or collection of religious or other rites.

If we look further at the idea of doing something *ceremoniously* or *religiously*, the difference between a routine and a ritual is the intention. Shifting a routine into a ritual *is* religious in that it is a conscientious "manifesting faithful devotion to an acknowledged ultimate reality" (Merriam-Webster.) What a powerful thought!

What does it look like when you apply it to real life? It is focusing your energy on what you want to experience. If you want to experience joy, it begins with creating the conditions required for it with your collective thoughts, words, and actions.

Commitment and openness are required. New ways of being can present challenges as we let go of the old ones. There will be times when we fall off, and that's okay. The commitment part is the willingness to get back on.

Being open in the *shift* to rituals is two-fold. The first is being open to incorporating different practices into your rituals, determining what's best for you. Your joy is unique, what works for others may not necessarily work for you. The other part is being open to any "downloads" (thoughts, realizations) that may come from what will become a mindful practice. Being present and in the moment.

Every task or routine can become a ritual. When I worked in education, I found it exceedingly difficult to detach emotionally and mentally from my work. I had poor boundaries, and could not turn off thoughts of students, meetings, and even my cell phone. I knew this wasn't sustainable, or healthy. As a way to support my intention of setting a boundary, and preparing my brain for it, I created a ritual.

Before leaving the house, I asked for spiritual support; that I have all I need to serve students and teachers, that I am shielded from taking on the pain and stress of others. Then I put on my lanyard as if it were a signal and shield that I was now "on." When I returned home, I said THANK YOU, expressing gratitude for my safety, my gift, and being able to serve. The practice of gratitude is a spiritual one, in that it allows us to take inventory of the blessings we've asked for, deepening our faith and connection.

When I removed the lanyard and hung it up, it signified that I was turning off, that my energy was no longer available for work. Goodbye, Dr. Boz, Behavior Specialist, hello Toya. Then I'd immediately take a 15-minute walk in my neighborhood or pace in my yard barefoot while I listened to music. After grounding myself or releasing stored energy from the day, I was now able to be present for myself and my family.

Because joy is dynamic, when I began working from home, I had to create a new ritual, a new signal to my mind and body that it was time to start my day. I still do my morning meditation and gratitude journal as I have for the last decade. Now my work-from-home ritual is French pressing my morning coffee while mantras play from my speaker. When I worked in schools, I used a timer on my coffee maker because my days started earlier. In my new role, I could invite joy into preparing my coffee: taking in the scent of ground coffee, swaying to rhythmic affirmations while my water boils, watching the hot, bubbling water fill the French press as my hands press the top down on the filter. Using the wait time it takes for my coffee to darken, I get my favorite mug, pour in the creamer, and sprinkle cinnamon, stirring it together. Then I pour my robust coffee over my mixture and continue stirring. I take that first sip. *Oh yeah, we are going to rock the day.* Just like that, I turned something mundane into something delightful. This is the shift from routine to rituals.

How do you transform a routine into a ritual? One step at a time. Pick one routine – morning and evening ones are best to start with as they are the most impactful parts of our day.

1. **How slow can you go?** Our schedules are packed, and our roles are many, so the idea of slowing down can be challenging. It's easy to equate your alarm clock with the start of a rat race. As sacrificial as this sounds, I encourage you to extend the amount of time you spend on a routine as you shape it into a ritual. This may mean getting up a little earlier, going to bed a little later, or even delegating some of your duties to others. Pick just one thing to do more slowly – showering, moisturizing, preparing your bed for sleep.

2. **How can you mindfully incorporate all or most of your senses?** The National Cancer Institute notes that aromatherapy (the use of essential oils from plants) affects the brain's limbic system, which is responsible for emotions and memory. Integrating the use of them influences mood, and perceived improvement of physical, emotional, and spiritual well-being.

   Other than your sense of smell, consider your sense of touch- what textures feel comforting or sensual to your skin? What sounds relax or invigorate you? Ocean waves, rain, smooth jazz? Experiment with streaming different types of music to include in your ritual.

3. **What can you add to enhance?** Outside of your senses, what can you add to your routine in the transition to a ritual? For example, part of my ritual before getting out of bed is meditation and stretching. Then, I say "Thank you" out loud when my feet hit the floor and immediately do a forward

fold (bending forward at the waist, legs straight, touching my toes). Then I do a sun salutation (face up, both hands outstretched, back slightly bent back). I find it far more beneficial than just pulling back the covers and standing up. What steps can you add to prayer or meditation? Perhaps it's breathwork or preparing a place to sit or kneel. What can you do before you turn on your laptop to flow into a ritual?

Again, this takes time, practice, and patience with yourself, but you can slowly create slight changes that will light up your life. Once you begin to master one ritual, you can begin creating more for other parts of your day. As the seasons change, or life happens, you experiment with new practices.

Affirmations for Joy

Joy is my unique experience.

I find joy in the journey.

I can actively choose joy at any moment.

I give myself permission to explore diverse ways of being.

I get to decide what brings me joy.

I find joy in playing.

I experience joyful and loving relationships.

I open myself to new joyful experiences.

I find joy in nature.

When I am grounded and grateful, I am joyful.

Who is Dr. Boz?

Dr. Boz supports others with creating space for themselves and their joy. Born Latoya Bosworth, she dubbed herself Brenda's Child at the age of twenty-one, in honor of her late mother Brenda Kay Swinton. Although she experienced early childhood and adolescent trauma, Latoya attributes her healing and evolution to writing as an outlet, strong mentors, spirituality, therapy and giving back. Between 2007 and 2019 she self-published twelve books, including five poetry collections, a memoir, a self-help book for young women, and several journals. She has written for several publications both online and in print.

After enrolling in her PhD program, her fellow educators began to refer to her as Dr. Boz. After earning her doctorate, Latoya embraced the name. Dr. Boz has worked in education and human services for over two decades as a teacher, consultant, workshop facilitator, adjunct professor, and curriculum creator. She has been empowering those to find and use their voice since establishing her arts and mentoring program, Keep Youth Dreaming and Striving (K.Y.D.S) in 2006. In 2020 she founded Got *H.E.R.S* Get More Life Coaching, specializing in confidence, joy, and purpose.

Dr. Boz is the mother of two sons and a grandmother to one. Dancing, self-fullness and spending time with people who fill her spirit with delight are favorite things to do when she is not following through on her next goal.

Other Titles by Dr. Boz

Quiet Strength Loud Confidence… Reflections and Realizations from a Free Black Woman (2021).

From Girl to Grown… A Guide to Living Unabashedly (2019).

The Right Amount of Sunshine… Cultivating Little Girls into Young Ladies (2010) by Brenda's Child

Learn more about Dr. Boz and her other titles at www.brendaschild.com

Sources

Arora, R., Mandal, M.K. (2023). Spirituality and Happiness: A Neuroscientific Perspective. In: Chetri, S., Dutta, T., Mandal, M.K., Patnaik, P. (eds) Understanding Happiness. Springer, Singapore. https://doi.org/10.1007/978-981-99-3493-5_2

Oschman JL, Chevalier G, Brown R. The effects of grounding (earthing) on inflammation, the immune response, wound healing, and prevention and treatment of chronic inflammatory and autoimmune diseases. J Inflamm Res. 2015 Mar 24;8:83-96. doi: 10.2147/JIR.S69656. PMID: 25848315; PMCID: PMC4378297.

PDQ® Integrative, Alternative, and Complementary Therapies Editorial Board. PDQ Aromatherapy With Essential Oils. Bethesda, MD: National Cancer Institute. Updated <01/13/2023>. Available

Robinson, Lawrence, Smith, Melinda Smith, Jeanne Segal, Shubin, Jennifer (2024). The importance of adult play/ https://www.helpguide.org/articles/mental-health/benefits-of-play-for-adults.htm

Wang J, Wei Z, Yao N, Li C, Sun L. Association Between Sunlight Exposure and Mental Health: Evidence from a Special Population Without Sunlight in Work. Risk Manag Healthc Policy. 2023 Jun 14;16:1049-1057. doi: 10.2147/RMHP.S420018. PMID: 37337544; PMCID: PMC10277019.lth/benefits-of-play-for-adults.htm

Made in United States
North Haven, CT
27 January 2025